For Heidi

D1518302

She doesn't want the worms

Ella no quiere los gusanos

A Mystery

By Karl Beckstrand
Illustrated by David Hollenbach

She doesn't want the Worms

Spanish vowels have one sound each: *a* = *ah* *e* = *eh* *i* = *ee* *o* = *oh* *u* = *oo*. Every vowel should be pronounced (except for the *u* after a *q* [*que* is pronounced *keh*]). In Spanish, the letter *j* is pronounced as an English *h* (and the letter *h* is silent), *ll* sounds like a *y* (or a *j* in some countries), and *ñ* has an *ny* sound (*año* sounds like *ah-nyo*).

Spanish nouns are masculine or feminine and are usually preceded by an article: *la* = feminine *the*; *el* = masculine *the*; *una* = feminine *a* or *one*; *un* = masculine *a* or *one*. Articles (and -s/-es after nouns) reflect plural: *las* = plural feminine *the*; *los* = plural masculine *the*; *unas* = feminine *some*; *unos* = masculine *some*. In Spanish, the accent is generally on the first or second syllable of simple words. Words with four or more syllables often have the accent on the third syllable. Variations occur with conjugation. If there's an accent mark—follow that!

Las combinaciones de letras en inglés pueden cambiar los sonidos por completo: *ck* se pronuncia como *k; wr* se pronuncia como *r; ee* se pronuncia *i; qu* se pronuncia *cu; ai* se pronuncia *ey; ll* se pronuncia *l;* y *gh* no tiene sonido en medio, y al final, de la mayoria de las palabras. El sonido de *ch* (de chico) se ocupa al comenzar palabras, en el medio, y al final también. Para pronunciar *sh*, manten la mandíbula cerrada y los labios abiertos; sopla aire entre los dientes (al añadir la vocal que le siga, si hay.) Para pronunciar *th*, pon la lengua entre los dientes de adelante (arriba y abajo) y sopla un poquito de aire sobre la lengua.

Los sustantivos en inglés no tienen género; se usa *the* para *la, el, las,* y *los*. Algunas palabras en inglés — a pesar de escribirse de forma diferente — terminan con el mismo sonido (se pronuncian como si se escribieran igual al final): *fleas* y *flees, touch* y *clutch, suit* y *cute, toad* y *node, nose* y *knows* y *goes*.

Premio Publishing & Gozo Books, LLC
Midvale, UT, USA
ISBN: 978-0-9776065-2-8

Text Copyright © 2011 Karl Beckstrand
Illustration Copyright © 2011 David Hollenbach
Library of Congress Catalog Number: 2010910827

Get this book in English-only, Spanish-only, or ebook versions. Pida este libro únicamente en español o ingles: Gozobooks.com. Discounts available for fundraising, bulk, school, and charitable donation orders. Descuentos para pedidos en volumen y para organizaciones educativas o caritativas.

Libros online GRATIS:

FREE online books & more:

Premiobooks.com

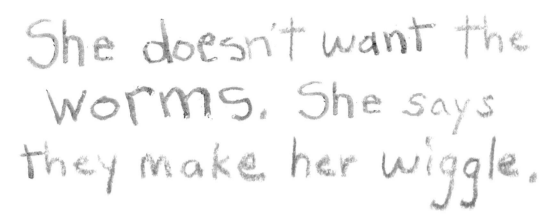

She doesn't want the worms. She says they make her wiggle.

Ella no quiere a los gusanos, no señor.
Ella dice que le hacen menearse mucho.

(Count each critter!)
(¡Cuenta cada bicho!)

She doesn't like the spiders. She thinks they'll make her giggle.

Las arañas, a ella, no le gustan. Piensa que tonta risa le causarán.

She will not clutch,
nor even touch,
the bumblebee I gave her.
The fly, she hates
(but tolerates it
...like a sour neighbor).

Que no, que no tocará,
ni asirá el abejorro
que le di.
Odia la mosca (pero la tolera
...al igual que la agria vecina.)

The snails in pails
—she shakes pigtails—
are not quite to her liking.

En los baldes
caracoles,
las coletas le
sacuden a disgusto
de su gusto.

Her wrinkled nose
means,
"the beetle goes!"
The scorpion sends
her hiking.

El *escarabajo* **se va**, denota su
nariz arrugada. El alacrán
la manda a pasear.

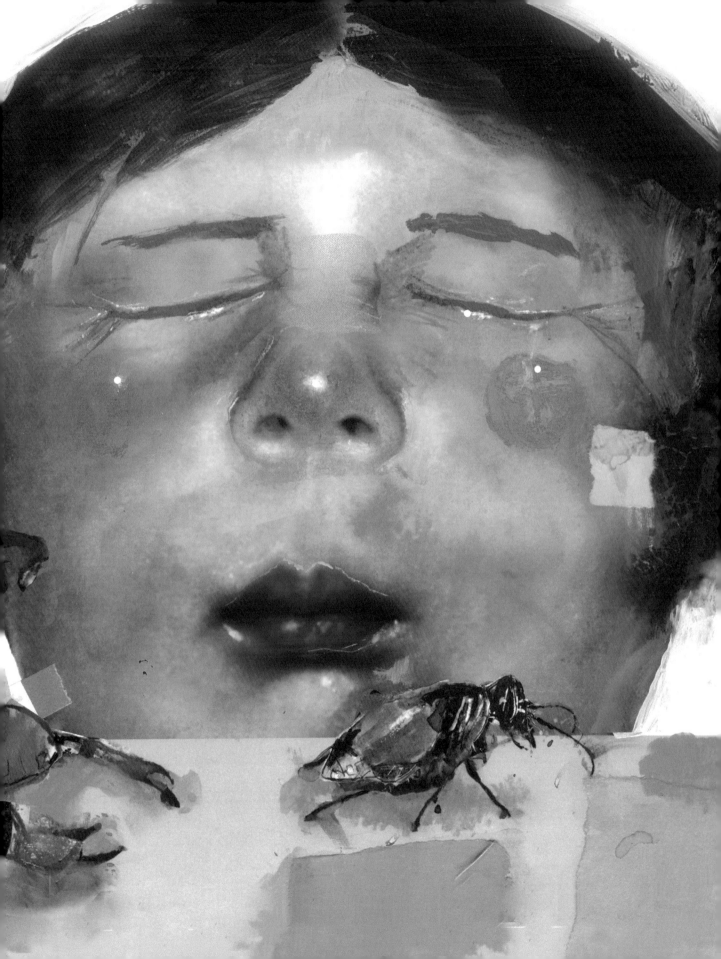

The charms of the
snake elude her.
the salamanders
mute her. the pollywogs
don't suit her.

De la serpiente, el encanto,
la elude. La hacen enmudecer
las salamandras.
De su agrado,
los renacuajos
no son.

The cockroach could be cuter.

Más bonita, la cucaracha podría ser.

She snubs the grubs.
She flees the fleas.
The caterpillar bores her.
The bat, the rat?
—She showed them her cat.

Ella rechaza las larvas.
Ella huye de las pulgas.
Le aburre la oruga.
¿El murciélago y la rata?
— Se los presentó al gato.

The slugs,
they just ignore her.

Las babosas, solo la ignoran.

The mantis
makes her
motionless. The
centipede is creepy.
The moth has got the wrong
address. The crickets
make her sleepy.

La mantis religiosa la paraliza.
Horripilante el ciempiés es.
La polilla se equivocó de
casa. Los grillos sueño,
sueño de verdad,
le dan.

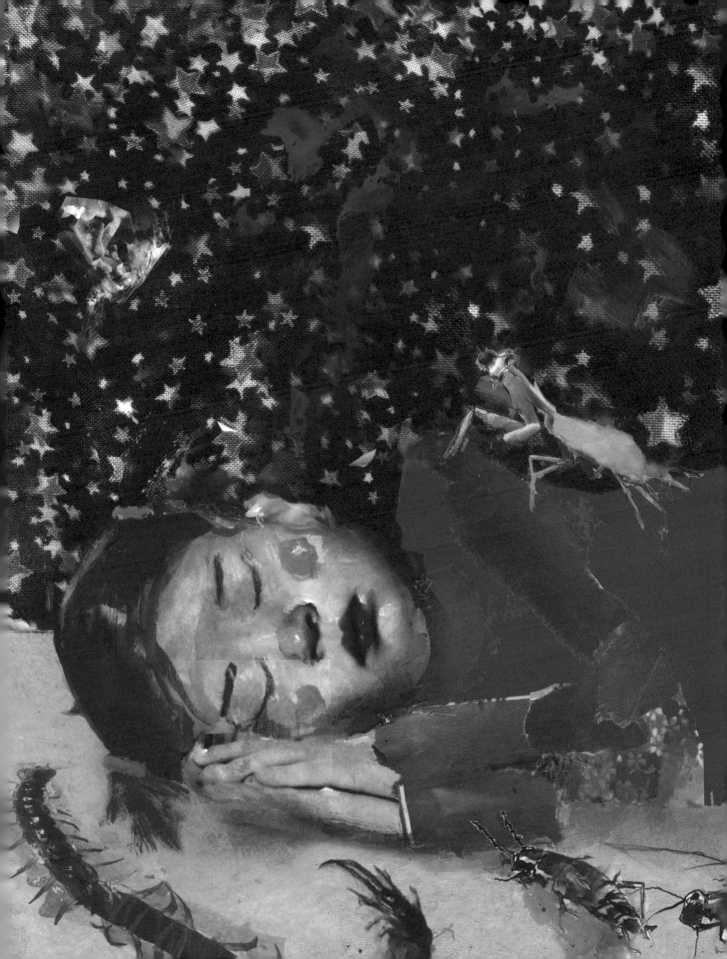

she likes
the dance
of the busy ants
across the
hummingbird feeder.

A ella le gusta la danza de
las trabajadoras hormigas
a través del bebedero de
los colibrí.

But the toad
with the node
made her hit the road.

Pero el sapo,
con su nódulo,
hizo que ella
a la fuga
se diera.

CPSIA information can be obtained
at www.ICGtesting.com
Printed in the USA
272044LV00005BA